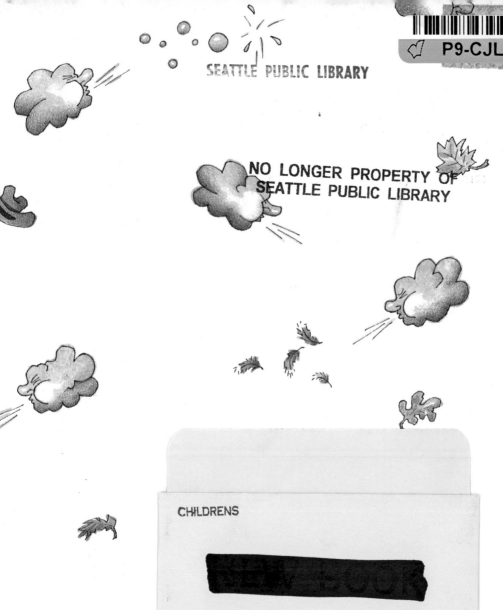

WINDY DAY

Stories and Poems

WINDY DAY

Stories and Poems

Edited by Caroline Feller Bauer

Illustrated by Dirk Zimmer

J. B. LIPPINCOTT

NEW YORK

Windy Day: Stories and Poems
Text copyright © 1988 by Caroline Feller Bauer
Illustrations copyright © 1988 by Dirk Zimmer
Printed in
the United States of America. For information address
J.B. Lippincott Junior Books, 10 East 53rd Street,
New York, N.Y. 10022. Published simultaneously in
Canada by Fitzhenry & Whiteside Limited, Toronto.

10 9 8 7 6 5 4 3 2 1
First Edition

Library of Congress Cataloging-in-Publication Data
Windy day.

Bibliography: p.
Summary: A collection of stories and poems about
wind by a variety of authors, with a bibliography,
a glossary of names for winds, and a few activities.
    1. Winds—Literary collections. [1. Winds—Literary
collections] I. Bauer, Caroline Feller. II. Zimmer,
Dirk, ill.
PZ5.W67 1988   808.8'036   86-42994
ISBN 0-397-32207-0
ISBN 0-397-32208-9 (lib. bdg.)

ACKNOWLEDGMENTS

Every effort has been made to trace ownership of all copyright material and to secure the necessary permissions to reprint these selections. In the event of any question arising as to the use of any material, the editor and the publisher, while expressing regret for any inadvertent error, will be happy to make the necessary correction in future printings. Thanks are due to the following for permission to reprint the copyrighted materials listed below:

Arnold Adoff, for "Late Past Bedtime" excerpted from the book *Tornado!* by Arnold Adoff. Copyright © 1977 by Arnold Adoff. Reprinted by permission of Delacorte Press. / Atheneum Publishers, Inc. for "Partners" from *Think of Shadows* by Lilian Moore. Copyright © 1975, 1980 Lilian Moore. / Atheneum Publishers, Inc. for "Until I Saw the Sea" from *I Feel the Same Way*. Copyright © 1967 Lilian Moore. / Atheneum Publishers, Inc. for "While You Were Chasing a Hat" from *Something New Begins* by Lilian Moore. Copyright © 1982 by Lilian Moore. / Atheneum Publishers, Inc. for "Wind" from *Catch Me a Wind* by Patricia Hubbell. Copyright © 1968 by Patricia Hubbell. / Bradbury Press, an affiliate of Macmillan Inc., for *Little Pieces of the West Wind* by Christian Garrison. Text copyright © 1975 by Christian Garrison. / Coward, McCann, & Geoghegan for *When the Wind Changed* by Ruth Park. Copyright © 1980 by Ruth Park. / Marchette Chute for "The Swing" from *Rhymes About Us*. Copyright © 1974. Reprinted by permission of Marchette Chute. / Padraic Colum for "I Saw the Wind Today" from *The Golden Journey*, compiled by Louise Bogan & William J. Smith, published by Contemporary Books, 1976. / Doubleday & Company, Inc. for "North Wind" by Mary O'Neill from *Winds*. Copyright © 1970 by Mary O'Neill. / E. P. Dutton, a division of New American Library, for "Wind on the Hill" from *Now We Are Six* by A. A. Milne. Copyright 1927 by E. P. Dutton, renewed 1955 by A. A. Milne. / Greenwillow Books (A Division of William Morrow & Company) for "I Am Flying!" from *The New Kid on the Block* by Jack Prelutsky. Copyright © 1984 by Jack Prelutsky. / Greenwillow Books (A Division of William Morrow & Company) for "I Do Not Mind You, Winter Wind" from *It's Snowing! It's Snowing!* by Jack Prelutsky. Copyright © 1984 by Jack Prelutsky. / Sidonie Matsner Gruenberg for "The Girl Who Could Think" from *Favorite Stories Old and New* by Sidonie Matsner Gruenberg. Copyright 1942, 1955 by Doubleday & Company, Inc. / Harper & Row, Publishers, Inc. for "Again and Again" from *Flower Moon Snow: A Book of Haiku* by Kazue Mizumura (Thomas Y. Crowell). Copyright © 1977 by Kazue Mizumura. / Harper & Row, Publishers, Inc. for "Days that the Wind Takes Over" and "Tree Birds" from *Near the Window Tree: Poems and Notes* by Karla Kuskin. Copyright © 1975 by Karla Kuskin. / Harper & Row, Publishers, Inc. for "Two Ways to Look at Kites" from *Cold Stars and Fireflies: Poems of the Four Seasons* by Barbara Juster Esbensen (Thomas Y. Crowell). Text copyright © 1984 by Barbara Juster Esbensen. / Harper & Row, Publishers, Inc. for "Wind Is a Cat" from *White Peaks and Green* by Ethel Romig Fuller (Harper & Row). / Felice Holman for "Sails, Gulls, Sky, Sea" from *I Hear You Smiling*. Published by Charles Scribner's Sons, 1973. Copyright Felice Holman. / M. Long for "The Window Cleaner." / New Directions Publishing Corp. for "The Term" from *Collected Earlier Poems* by William Carlos Williams. Copyright © 1938 by New Directions Publishing Corp. / Marian Reiner, Permissions Consultant, for *Crick! Crack!* from *Blackberry Ink* by Eve Merriam. Text copyright © 1983 by Eve Merriam. / Marian Reiner, Permissions Consultant, for "Texas Norther" from *The Malibu and Other Poems* by Myra Cohn Livingston. Copyright © 1972 by Myra Cohn Livingston. / The James Reeves Estate for "The Wind" from *James Reeves: The Complete Poems* © James Reeves Estate. / Susan Alton Schmeltz for "Paper Dragons." / Smithsonian Institution Press for "The Black Snake Wind Came to Me" from *Twenty-sixth Annual Report of the Bureau of American Ethnology to the Secretary of the Smithsonian Institution, 1904-5*. "The Pima Indian" by Frank Russell. Smithsonian Institution, Washington, D.C. 1908. / Grace Cornell Tall for "Winter Is a Wolf" from *Cricket Magazine*, January 1985, Volume 12, #5. / Paul Walker for "Leaves." / Wesleyan University Press for "The Bagel" from *Rescue the Dead* by David Ignatow. Copyright © 1966 by David Ignatow.

Just for Judy Schoenstein
Friends thirty years later

Contents

x

Who Has Seen the Wind?

CHRISTINA ROSSETTI

Who has seen the wind?
  Neither I nor you:
But when the leaves hang trembling,
  The wind is passing through.

Who has seen the wind?
  Neither you nor I:
But when the leaves bow down their heads,
  The wind is passing by.

WINDY DAY

Stories and Poems

The Girl Who Could Think

A CHINESE TALE

Lotus-Blossom and Moon-Flower think only of parties and merrymaking. Will they be able to solve two impossible riddles?

Lotus-Blossom and Moon-Flower were two young girls who lived long ago in the country of China. Now Lotus-Blossom and Moon-Flower were very good friends and they loved to go to parties.

Sometimes their parents would worry about them. "Oh, dear," the mother of Lotus-Blossom would say, "our daughters never think of anything but parties and merry-making and pretty clothes."

"I know," the mother of Moon-Flower would agree; "but some day they will get married and settle down and think of more important things."

When Lotus-Blossom and Moon-Flower grew up they married two brothers who lived in a village some distance away. After the wedding celebrations were over, the two young men brought their wives home to live with their mother.

3

Lotus-Blossom and Moon-Flower were very happy in their new home. They loved their young husbands and they loved their old mother-in-law and they were glad that they could live together in the same house.

But every little while they wanted to go back to their old village and go to parties and make merry with their old friends. They were forever coming to their mother-in-law and saying: "Honored lady, we pray you, let us go and pay a visit to the village of our childhood."

Now their mother-in-law was very fond of Lotus-Blossom and Moon-Flower. Her two daughters-in-law were good and kind and obedient. They would bring her tea whenever she asked them to, and three times a day they would serve her rice on little red lacquer tables. But she didn't like their going away every little while just for some parties and merrymaking. She thought they should stay and take care of their husbands and think of more important things.

So one day she said to herself, "I will put a stop to this once and for all." The very next time that Lotus-Blossom and Moon-Flower asked to go home, the mother-in-law replied: "Yes, my daughters, go. Go and enjoy yourselves. Go as soon as you like. But remember this. You must bring

4

me two gifts when you return, the only two things that I want, or else you shall not return to your husbands and your home."

"We will bring you anything you like!" the two daughters-in-law replied. "Tell us what presents you want and we shall bring them."

"Very well," said the mother-in-law, "listen carefully. You, Lotus-Blossom, must bring me some fire wrapped in paper. And you, Moon-Flower, must bring me the wind in a paper."

The two girls were so anxious to be gone that they did *not* listen carefully. Without thinking they replied, "Oh yes, honored lady, we will do just as you say! We will bring you anything you want!"

They said good-bye to their mother-in-law and they said good-bye to their husbands. Then off they went down the road toward the village of their childhood, chatting merrily all the way.

All of a sudden Lotus-Blossom remembered what her mother-in-law had asked her to bring: some fire wrapped in paper. Surely that was impossible! And if she did not bring this present to her mother-in-law, Lotus-Blossom could never see her husband again. She sat down by the

5

roadside and started to cry as if her heart would break.

Then it came over Moon-Flower, too, that she would never see *her* husband again. For surely it was impossible to bring the wind in a paper! So she sat beside her sister-in-law by the roadside, and the two girls cried and cried as if their hearts would break.

Just then a young girl working in a nearby rice field saw them. She came over to Lotus-Blossom and Moon-Flower and said to them, "Crying will not make things better. Tell me your trouble and perhaps I can help you."

They told her as best they could of all that had

happened and the girl said to them, "Surely you have been foolish, but perhaps we can still find a way out. Let us think."

Now Lotus-Blossom and Moon-Flower had never even dreamed of thinking. All their lives they had let other people think for them. But if this girl could think, they said to themselves, why, so could they! So they went off with her, across the fields, to her father's house.

The three sat down on the front porch and tried to think. But the more they thought, the sadder Lotus-Blossom and Moon-Flower became, for they could not think of any way to carry fire or wind in a paper.

Suddenly their new friend sprang to her feet and ran into her father's house. In a few moments she came back carrying a lantern in her hand. It was made entirely of paper and inside the lantern a candle was burning brightly.

"Look!" she said. "Here is fire wrapped in paper."

"Oh, how wonderful!" Lotus-Blossom exclaimed. "Just the present for me to bring back to my mother-in-law."

But poor Moon-Flower was as unhappy as ever. It still seemed impossible that a way could be found to bring back the wind in a paper. All of a sudden their new friend sprang

7

to her feet again and ran into her father's house. This time she brought back a paper fan. She waved it back and forth in front of Moon-Flower, and Moon-Flower felt the wind in her face.

"See!" the girl said. "Wind in a paper!"

"Oh, how wonderful!" Moon-Flower exclaimed. "Just the present for my mother-in-law. Now I can return home, too!"

The two girls thanked their new friend again and again and then started back up the road toward home.

8

When their mother-in-law saw the two girls coming up the road she went to the door to meet them.

"What is this?" she asked sternly. "Are these two girls who do not obey their mother-in-law?"

"No indeed, honored lady!" the two girls cried. "We have brought you the presents for which you asked."

Lotus-Blossom held up the lantern for her mother-in-law to see and Moon-Flower waved the fan back and forth, sending the wind against her face.

"Ah," the honored lady cried. "I see someone has done some thinking. Welcome home, my daughters. Let us have a cup of tea, with the lantern lighting the table and the paper fan to cool us."

The Wind

JAMES REEVES

I can get through a doorway without any key,
And strip the leaves from the great oak tree.

I can drive storm-clouds and shake tall towers,
Or steal through a garden and not wake the flowers.

Seas I can move and ships I can sink;
I can carry a house-top or the scent of a pink.

When I am angry I can rave and riot;
And when I am spent, I lie quiet as quiet.

Days that the Wind Takes Over

KARLA KUSKIN

Days that the wind takes over
Blowing through the gardens
Blowing birds out of the street trees
Blowing cats around corners
Blowing my hair out
Blowing my heart apart
Blowing high in my head
Like the sea sound caught in a shell.
One child put her thin arms around the wind
And they went off together.
Later the wind came back
Alone.

The Wind and the Moon

GEORGE MACDONALD

Said the Wind to the Moon,
"I will blow you out;
   You stare
   In the air
   Like a ghost in a chair
Always looking what I am about.
I hate to be watched—I'll blow you out."

Crick! Crack!

EVE MERRIAM

Crick! Crack!
Wind at my back.

Snit! Snat!
Snatched off my hat.

Whew! Whew!
It blew and it blew.

Snapped at my ears,
Flapped at my shoes,

And now I've got only
One mitten to lose.

I Do Not Mind You, Winter Wind

JACK PRELUTSKY

I do not mind you, Winter Wind
when you come whirling by,
to tickle me with snowflakes
drifting softly from the sky.

I do not even mind you
when you nibble at my skin,
scrambling over all of me
attempting to get in.

But when you bowl me over
and I land on my behind,
then I must tell you, Winter Wind,
I mind...I really mind!

Leaves

PAUL WALKER

The leaves fall
Like big pennies,
And the sidewalk catches them.

Wind Is a Cat

ETHEL ROMIG FULLER

Wind is a cat
  That prowls at night,
Now in a valley,
  Now on a height,

Pouncing on houses
  Till folks in their beds
Draw all the covers
  Over their heads.

It sings to the moon,
  It scratches at doors;
It lashes its tail
  Around chimneys and roars.

It claws at the clouds
  Till it fringes their silk;
It laps up the dawn
  Like a saucer of milk;

16

Then, chasing the stars
　　To the tops of the firs,
Curls down for a nap
　　And purrs and purrs.

The Swing

MARCHETTE CHUTE

The wind blows strong and the swing rides free,
And up in the swing is me, is me,
    And the world goes rushing by,
And one of these days I'll swing so far
I'll go way up where the sea birds are
    And plant my feet on the sky.

18

Again and Again

KAZUE MIZUMURA

Again and again,
The wind wipes away the clouds
And shines up the moon.

19

Make a paper fan, and you have wind in paper. Accordion pleat an 8″ x 10″ sheet of paper. Open it up and hold one end to make a fan.

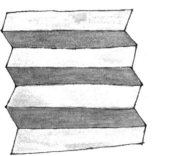 

To determine wind direction, wet your finger and stick it up high in the air. The side of your finger that feels cold and dries first indicates the direction from which the wind is blowing.

Make a parachute to float on the wind.

You need: a square of cloth

           4 pieces of string, each cut about the length
               of one side of cloth

           a paper clip

Tie one end of a piece of string to each corner of the cloth. Tie the other end of each string to the paper clip. Throw the parachute into the air or drop it from a high place—the top of a slide or jungle gym. Watch the wind float your parachute to the ground.

Little Pieces of the West Wind

CHRISTIAN GARRISON

A clever old man loses his socks and makes a bargain with the wild and reckless West Wind.

Once there was a clever old man who had lost his socks.

"I know a way to get back my socks," said the clever old man.

He opened his door and all of the windows and then sat down to wait for the West Wind.

That afternoon the West Wind came blustering through the open door and windows of the cabin.

Just as the West Wind entered, the clever old man jumped up, slammed shut the door, and closed all of the windows with a bang.

"HA!" he said to the West Wind. "I have caught you!"

Sure enough. The wild West Wind blew and bounced about inside the cabin, but was unable to get away.

"What do you want of me, old man?" bellowed the West Wind.

"I have lost my socks, and I want you to find them for me," said the clever old man.

"I am the wild and reckless West Wind! I work for no man!" wailed the West Wind.

He swelled and blew and crashed against the window, but could not find so much as a tiny crack to seep through.

The clever old man chuckled, and the West Wind finally agreed to do as he asked. "But I do not trust you, West Wind. So I will keep a little piece of you here with me until you return with my socks."

With that, the clever old man pulled off a piece of the West Wind and wrapped it in a rug. Then he opened the window, and what was left of the mighty West Wind blew away to look for the clever old man's socks.

Soon the West Wind came upon a woodchopper who was wearing socks on his hands. "You make a funny sight with socks on your *hands*," said the West Wind with a whistle. "Who cares?" grunted the woodchopper without looking up. "Where are your gloves?" asked the West Wind. "Lost," grumbled the woodchopper. "Let me have those socks!" hissed the West Wind. "No," said the woodchopper, "not unless you find my gloves."

The West Wind sputtered and howled. At last he agreed to do as the woodchopper asked. "But I do not trust

24

you, West Wind. So I will keep a little piece of you here with me until you return with my gloves."

With that, the woodchopper chopped off a piece of the West Wind and put it inside a hollow log and stopped up the hole, and what was left of the mighty West Wind blew through the trees to look for the woodchopper's gloves.

Soon the West Wind came upon a gypsy who was wearing a pair of gloves on her head. "You make a funny sight with gloves on your *head*," wailed the West Wind. "Goodness me! Do I?" giggled the gypsy, blushing from head to toe. "Have you no scarf?" the West Wind asked. "I cannot find it anywhere," said she. "I would like to have those gloves," said the West Wind. "I should say not, you silly wind!" snapped the gypsy. "But if you bring me back my scarf, then you may have these gloves."

The West Wind shook the trees and rustled the leaves, but finally agreed to do as she asked. "But I do not trust you, West Wind. So I will keep a little piece of you here with me until you return with my scarf."

With that, the gypsy pinched off a piece of the West Wind and placed it inside her tea tin where she kept her tea leaves, and what was left of the once mighty West Wind wandered away to look for the gypsy's scarf.

Soon the West Wind came upon a sheep who had a scarf around his leg. "You make a funny sight with that scarf around your *leg*," wheezed the West Wind. "BAAAAA!" cried the sheep. "Why are you wearing that scarf?" the West Wind asked. "Because I have lost my blue ribbon I won at the fair," sobbed the sheep. "Give me that scarf, sheep," said the West Wind. "NOOOOO!" said the sheep. "Go find my blue ribbon, and then I shall gladly give you this scarf."

The West Wind was too tired by now to fuss and fume, and he agreed to do as the sheep asked. "But I do not trust you, West Wind. So I will keep a little piece of you here with me until you return with my blue ribbon."

With that, the sheep bit off a piece of the West Wind and stuffed it under his haystack to keep. And what was left of the once mighty West Wind floated off to look for the sheep's blue ribbon.

So the West Wind came upon a bird who had a blue ribbon in her tail. "You make a funny sight with that blue ribbon in your *tail*," whispered the West Wind. "You would too!" chirped the bird. "Have you lost your tail feather?" the West Wind asked. "Yes indeed!" sang she. "May I please have that blue ribbon, bird?" whined the West Wind. "You may not!" said the bird. "Find my tail feather, and you may have this blue ribbon."

All the West Wind could do was sigh and agree to do as the bird asked. "But I do not trust you, West Wind. So I will keep a little piece of you here with me until you return with my tail feather."

With that, the bird pecked off a piece of the West Wind and stuck it under her nest to keep.

By now the West Wind was nothing more than a puff of breeze as he went to look for the bird's tail feather.

At last the West Wind came upon a little girl who was playing with a feather. "Please give me your feather, young lady," sighed the West Wind. "I can barely hear you. Why do you whisper, and who are you?" the little girl asked. "The mighty West Wind," said he. "Why, you are nothing more than a tiny puff of breeze," she replied. "That is because others have pulled, chopped, pinched, bitten, and pecked away little pieces of me," the West Wind whispered. "I will give you this feather, West Wind. But will you come back to see me every afternoon to cool me off and keep me company?"

He was too weak to refuse. So the tiny puff of breeze that once was the mighty West Wind took the feather and went away to keep all of the bargains he had made that day.

The bird got back her tail feather and returned the blue ribbon and the little piece of wind.

The sheep got back his blue ribbon and returned the scarf and the little piece of wind.

The gypsy got back her scarf and returned the pair of gloves and the little piece of wind.

The woodchopper got back his gloves and returned the pair of socks and the little piece of wind.

The West Wind was growing mighty and strong again by the time he arrived at the cabin of the clever old man. "Come out, old man! I have returned with your socks, and I want the piece of me you are keeping!"

Gladly the clever old man unwrapped the rug and let out the piece of wind he was keeping there.

And that made the West Wind whole again.

The clever old man chuckled and sat down to put on his socks as the mighty West Wind blustered away.

I Saw the Wind Today

PADRAIC COLUM

I saw the wind today:
I saw it in the pane
Of glass upon the wall:
A moving thing,—'twas like
No bird with widening wing,
No mouse that runs along
The meal bag under the beam.

I think it like a horse,
All black, with frightening mane,
That springs out of the earth,
And tramples on his way.
I saw it in the glass,
The shaking of a mane:
A horse that no one rides!

Two Ways to Look at Kites

BARBARA JUSTER ESBENSEN

1.
Sky-flowers!
They bloom and toss
on tight stems
invisibly rooted
in our hands.

2.
In the blue air
schools of kites
dive and flash—paper fish!
My kite struggles
to leap free
pulls
my arms out straight
but I reel him in
still fighting   zigzagging
against the currents
of wind.

North Wind

MARY O'NEILL

Is your father
A long, sharp, glittering knife?
And did he take the bluest,
Coldest, tallest iceberg for a wife?
Did they feed you
Sharp little slivers of ice
And powdered tundra mixed
With frozen mice?
Was your mother proud
When you puffed your cheeks
And uttered your first
Howls and shrieks?
Did they teach you that any
Day was lost
Unless it carried
A chilling frost?

Did you learn that
To bite and freeze
Was better manners
Than saying: "Please"?
Did your father say:
"Go blacken leaves,
Run down collars,
Up skirts and sleeves"?
Did your mother say:
"Go nip some noses
And freeze the water
In firemen's hoses"?
Is your pencil an icicle?
Why do you cry
Sometimes in the night
Between the roof and sky?

The Black Snake Wind

TRADITIONAL PIMA INDIAN POEM

The Black Snake Wind came to me,
The Black Snake Wind came to me.
Came and wrapped itself about
Came here running with its song.

Sails, Gulls, Sky, Sea

FELICE HOLMAN

Sails
    against the wind
        like gulls—
Gulls
    like sails
        against the sky—
Sky
    a net
        above the sea—
Sea
    like time
        a long blue line.

Partners

LILIAN MOORE

This is the wind's doing,
this clothesline
dance—

shirttails twirling,
sleeves
clapping, thigh-slapping,
jeans stepping high.

What flapping, snapping,
whirling
to the wind's whistle!

This is the sun's doing,
these shadows
leaping, twisting,
prancing,
partners dancing
to the same tune.

Until I Saw the Sea

LILIAN MOORE

Until I saw the sea
I did not know
that wind
could wrinkle water so.

I never knew
that sun
could splinter a whole sea of blue.

Nor
did I know before,
a sea breathes in and out
upon a shore.

late past bedtime

arnold adoff

we are meeting

         around

the kitchen

   table

the wind is blowing from the west again

   and the creaking branches of the

                 big

    tree in the yard

        make

          their

       moans

the windows rattle

   like another storm

is coming

     and everything outside

      is much too   loud

     for

       bedtime

Wind

PATRICIA HUBBELL

I draw the hood of the wind about me.
    I button it closer, grasping at its corners.
The wind curves nearer, clutching my hair.
    I reach a hand to straighten it; it slides
And leaves my hair disheveled.
    I stand and the wind becomes my dress;
I move and the wind moves with me.
    Clothed by the wind, under the oak trees,
I feel the need for tallness.
    The wind surrounds me, permeates me.
It stretches my soul.

I Am Flying!

JACK PRELUTSKY

I am flying! I am flying!
I am riding on the breeze,
I am soaring over meadows,
I am sailing over seas,
I ascend above the cities
where the people, small as ants,
cannot sense the keen precision
of my aerobatic dance.

I am flying! I am flying!
I am climbing unconfined,
I am swifter than the falcon,
and I leave the wind behind,
I am swooping, I am swirling
in a jubilant display,
I am brilliant as a comet
blazing through the Milky Way.

I am flying! I am flying!
I am higher than the moon,
still, I think I'd best be landing,
and it cannot be too soon,
for some nasty information
has lit up my little brain—
I am flying! I am flying!
but I fly without a plane.

Wind is moving air.

A weather vane shows which direction the wind is blowing.

A windmill uses wind to produce power.

Seeds are carried by the wind and spread plants and trees. Pick a dandelion that has gone to seed and blow. Watch the wind carry the seeds away.

Sounds and smells travel with the wind. If an animal is "downwind" from you, it can smell your presence.

When the Wind Changed

RUTH PARK

Josh can do lots of things, but he's best at making faces. One day he makes the best face of all, but suddenly the wind changes.

There was this boy named Josh. He could do lots of things. There was one thing he could do best of all. He could make faces. He found out how good he was at making faces because of the dog next door.

The dog did not like cats, sea gulls, or big or little people. Most of all he did not like Josh. He always hoped that Josh would come over the fence, and then he could bite him.

One day Josh's ball flew over the fence. Josh climbed up to see if he could get it. There it lay in the middle of the dog's garden. The dog made a terrible noise. "Good dog," said Josh. "Want a nice bone, doggie?" The dog made another noise that Josh understood very well. The bone the dog wanted was Josh's leg bone.

Josh made a face at him. It was just an ordinary awful face. But the dog's tail drooped. His ears went flat. He ran

onto his porch. He growled as Josh climbed over the fence, but as Josh was still making the face, he dared not come closer.

When Josh got back to his own place with the ball, he went inside. There was his grandmother reading the newspaper. "Look, Gran," said Josh. "I can make a face that scares dogs." Grandmother looked up, gave a screech, and batted Josh over the head with her newspaper. Josh was surprised and pleased. He went to the mirror to have a look at his dog-and-Gran-scaring face. It did not seem very special.

"I can do better than that," he thought. Every day he practiced. He discovered more and more awful faces. He tried them out on the mailman.

48

He tried them on his mother. His mother was not a screecher, but she did ask him not to try his faces on the people in the street because it would not be good for Dad's business.

Dad was a teller at the bank down the street. He was an important person and always wore a very white shirt. Dad was a hard person to upset.

When Josh tried the most awful of his faces on him, all he did was to look thoughtfully at Josh and say: "I don't know if you've heard, Josh, but if you're making a face and the wind changes it will stay that way." "Ho ho," said Josh, but that didn't upset his father either.

Josh went on practicing faces. Then one day he made the best face of all. It was hideous. It almost scared Josh himself. Suddenly the wind changed. His face stayed the

way it was. He tried to squash it back into shape. He heaved up under his chin. He pressed on top of his head. He squeezed and pummeled his cheeks. It was no use. Josh went outside and climbed the fence. The dog next door saw him. It fell down and went on like a howling jelly. Josh could see that if his face never changed back, life would be very awkward.

He decided to go ask his Dad what to do. After all, Dad had known what would happen when the wind changed. He might know some more.

As Josh was a thoughtful boy, he put on his cowboy

hat and tied a red hanky around his face. This was so he would not scare people in the street.

When he reached the bank, a robbery was going on. People had their hands up, and a holdup man was waving a gun at Dad.

Josh was so worried about his face that he noticed nothing.

He marched up to the counter, pulled off his hat and hanky, and said: "Look, Dad!" The holdup man saw him first. He had a stocking over his head, but even through the stocking Josh could see his face turn snow white. He made a funny noise and dropped his gun.

Quick as light, Dad grabbed it up and bopped him with it. Just as he did, the wind changed once more. Josh's face smoothed out, and he looked like an ordinary boy. Dad and Josh were both heroes. They had stopped a robbery and saved the bank hundreds of thousands of dollars.

That night Dad was on the news program on TV. He explained what had happened. He said that Josh had decided he would never make awful faces again.

"Funny thing," said Dad. "When I was a boy, I was very good at making faces. This was my best one. Just look at this."

Just then the wind changed.

Wind on the Hill

A. A. MILNE

No one can tell me,
  Nobody knows,
Where the wind comes from,
  Where the wind goes.

The Window Cleaner

M. LONG

When I grow up I want to be
A window cleaning man
And make the windows in our street
As shiny as I can.
I'll put my ladder by the wall
And up the steps I'll go
But when I'm up there with my pail
I hope the wind won't blow.

Winter Is a Wolf

GRACE CORNELL TALL

Winter is a
   drowsy wolf

            full of summer sleep.
            He'll awaken and arise
            when the hunger in his eyes
            grows ravenous and deep.

Winter is a
   clever wolf

            You will see him creep
            down the Wind's way
            sly and slow
            in a suit of fleecy snow
            pretending he's a sheep.

Winter is a
magic wolf

no man-made cage can keep.
Crouching low on padded paws,
licking his enormous jaws,
earthward he will leap.

Tree Birds

KARLA KUSKIN

Tree birds
Light like leaves
On trees.
Twitter,
Glitter,
Ease into a passing breeze
And leave for greener trees.

Paper Dragons

SUSAN ALTON SCHMELTZ

In March, kites bite the wind
and shake their paper scales.
They strain against their fiber chains
to free their dragon tails.

The Term

WILLIAM CARLOS WILLIAMS

A rumpled sheet
of brown paper
about the length

and apparent bulk
of a man was
rolling with the

wind slowly over
and over in
the street as

a car drove down
upon it and
crushed it to

the ground. Unlike
a man it rose
again rolling

with the wind over
and over to be as
it was before.

Texas Norther

MYRA COHN LIVINGSTON

I'll buy me a wind today.
It's fall, so why not buy a wind,

a noisy one to stir up my head
and make my arms go round like

branches pushing, my body swaying
like a trunk, an angry wind

with cotton-picking fingers
snatching the old green

of summer, stripping the trees
and chasing dead leaves down the street

to the wind market, at a bargain
price of fifty mph for a blue norther.

The Bagel

DAVID IGNATOW

I stopped to pick up the bagel
rolling away in the wind,
annoyed with myself
for having dropped it
as if it were a portent.
Faster and faster it rolled,
with me running after it
bent low, gritting my teeth,
and I found myself doubled over
and rolling down the street
head over heels, one complete somersault
after another like a bagel
and strangely happy with myself.

While You Were Chasing a Hat

LILIAN MOORE

The wind
that whirled
your hat
away

furled a flag
filled a sail

raced a boat
tugged a kite

tweaked its tail

towed a cloud
rode a wave

chased some crows
flung them far

strummed on a
telephone wire
guitar

thrumming a tune
mile on mile
all the while you

were
chasing
a hat.

Weather saying: When the wind is out of the east,
'Tis good for neither man nor beast.
But when the wind is out of the west,
It sends every man the very best.

LOCAL WINDS

Some local winds that blow from the mountains or the desert are famous for bringing unusual weather.

Sirocco blows from the Sahara to the countries in the Mediterranean.

The *Santa Ana* blows from the desert across Southern California.

A *Chinook* comes from the Rocky Mountains and blows over Western Canada, Oregon, and Washington.

A *Foehn* blows from the mountains into Austria and Germany.

A *Monsoon* brings dry pleasant weather to India in the winter and torrential rains in the summer.

A *Mistral* comes from the Alps and blows on France.

Something to Read

PICTURE BOOKS

Brave Irene by William Steig. Illustrated by author. Farrar Straus &
  Giroux. *The wind swirls around Irene as she bravely struggles
  through a storm.*

Brother to the Wind by Mildred Pitts Walker. Illustrated by Diane and
  Leo Dillon. Lothrop, Lee & Shepard. *Emeke uses the wind to fly.*

The Girl Who Loved the Wind by Jane Yolen. Illustrated by Ed Young.
  Crowell. *The wind reveals the world to Princess Danina.*

Iva Dunnit and the Big Wind by Carol Purdy. Illustrated by Steven
  Kellogg. Dial. *Iva and her six children survive a wind storm.*

Jack and the Whoopee Wind by Mary Calhoun. Illustrated by Dick
  Gackenbach. Morrow. *Jack tries all sorts of schemes to stop the
  constantly blowing wind.*

Lullaby of the Wind by Karen Whiteside. Illustrated by Kazue
  Mizumura. Harper & Row. *The wind sings a nighttime lullaby
  telling everyone to go to sleep.*

Miss Rumphius by Barbara Cooney. Illustrated by the author. Viking. *The wind gives Miss Rumphius an idea "to make the world more beautiful."*

A Net to Catch the Wind by Margaret Greaves. Illustrated by Stephen Gammell. Harper & Row. *Can you really catch the wind... or a horse?*

Sailing with the Wind by Thomas Locker. Illustrated by the author. Dial. *Elizabeth sails through a storm with her Uncle Jack.*

Tornado! by Arnold Adoff. Illustrated by Ronald Himler. Delacorte. *The author describes the violence of a tornado; the artist shows a family experiencing it.*

When the Wind Blew by Margaret Wise Brown. Illustrated by Geoffrey Hayes. Harper & Row. *Trouble comes to an old woman and her cats on the day the wind blows.*

The Wind Blew by Pat Hutchins. Puffin. *The wind steals an umbrella from Mr. White, a balloon from Priscilla, and a judge's wig.*

LONGER BOOKS

Belinda's Hurricane by Elizabeth Winthrop. Illustrated by Wendy Watson. Dutton. *Granny May and Belinda prepare for a hurricane on Fox Island.*

The Cay by Theodore Taylor. Doubleday. *Phillip and Timothy are shipwrecked on an island.*

Goodbye, My Island by Jean Rogers. Illustrated by Rie Munoz. Greenwillow. *Twelve-year-old Esther tells of her last stormy, windy winter on Kind Island, Alaska.*

Kites for Kids by Burton and Rita Marks. Illustrated by Lisa Campbell Ernst. Lothrop, Lee & Shepard. *Use the wind to fly the kite you make yourself.*

The Lion and the Ostrich Chicks by Ashley Bryan. Illustrated by the author. Atheneum. *The wind carries our secret.*

Mary Poppins by P. L. Travers. Illustrated by Mary Shepard. Harcourt, Brace Jovanovich. *When Mary Poppins arrives with the East Wind she brings adventure.*

On the Banks of Plum Creek by Laura Ingalls Wilder. Illustrated by Garth Williams. Harper & Row. *Laura and her family find life exciting in pioneer America.*

When the Wind Blows Hard by Denise Gosliner Orenstein. Illustrated by Linda Strauss Edwards. Addison–Wesley. *Shawn adjusts to life in Klawood, Alaska.*

Windmills: An Old-New Energy Source by Lucile McDonald. Illustrated by Helen Hawkes Battey. Lodestar Books, Elsevier/ Nelson. *Find out how to use the wind to produce energy.*

The Wizard of Oz by L. Frank Baum. Illustrated by Michael Hague. Holt. *Dorothy and her dog, Toto, are swept by the wind to the Land of Oz.*

Index